# How to <u>Really</u> Beat Computer Games

Parts One and Two
Plus a collection of articles on beating Computer Games

John Bates Clare

ISBN: 978-0-9560927-3-1

# DEDICATION

To my parents Michael and Dorothy, thank you for always being there and supporting me.

## Introduction.

I have been playing computer games since I was eight years old. One Christmas I was given the Astro Wars video game. My first computer was a Commodore Vic-20 with a cassette recorder that took forever to load the games or programs. The first game I ever remember playing was Motormania, where you had to drive the wrong way down a road and avoid oncoming traffic. I was hooked. I next got a Commodore 64, slightly faster but still you could make a cup of tea whilst waiting for it to load games. I had the C64 for years and eventually got all the add ons like a disk drive and a printer etc.

My first console was a Sega Megadrive, I purchased the F1 game and was soon after a bit of practice, winning races and championships. Then when I started to earn money I bought a PS1. I was probably the first person in the country to own the F1 game. I bought the console, then could not resist the F1 game, but Dixon's would not let it out of the shop as it was due to be released the next day. So I had to go back and I was the first person in the shop the next morning.

I now have a PS2/Nintendo Wii and a PC and use both for gaming.

As a hobby I collect those 8-bit computers on which I first learned basic on and build them into systems that we all dreamed of owning and sell them on eBay.

This is not intended to be a massive technical manual, but a collection of tips and hints that I have picked up during almost 23 years of gaming.

Anyway enough about me, let's get down to business.

Good luck and I hope your enjoy this work.

## How a computer runs a game.

Unlike humans, the computer does not have a brain and therefore must rely on the code the programmer puts into his/her programme.

The code consists of commands/routines and sub-routines. When the programme is run those commands turn into actions which the computer will not deviate from. Let's take the Hello World programme to give you an idea.

10 Print "Hello World"
20 End

The user runs the program and the words Hello World are displayed on the screen, that's it, nothing else.

So, our memory is crucially important to us. To give you another example, the Star Wars Trilogy Arcade game based on the episodes A New Hope, Empire Strikes back and Return of the Jedi. In A New Hope, you are in a battle with tie fighters and one x-wing is being tailed by a tie fighter. If you shoot the tie fighter you get a nice message saying "Thanks, that was too close", if you hit the x-wing the message is "Hey, I'm your friend". R2D2 and CP3O appear at the same points in Empire Strikes Back as do the storm troopers. In Return of the Jedi the same storm trooper chases the same Ewok. So I think you are now getting the picture, our memory gives us an advantage.

The next step is to read your manual. You may have seen the film War Games about a teenager called David who accidentally hacks into the Pentagon war simulation computer and nearly starts world war three. In order to get the secret password that the original designer created.

David collects all the information about the machines creator, this does not help much until his friend watches a video of the programmes creator and his son, and on a hunch David tries typing in the sons name and bingo they unwittingly start Global Thermonuclear War playing the Russians. You do not need to go to this trouble, all you need is your game manual.

Study the manual well. Another example: I was struggling with Desert Strike on the mega drive when I first played it. I kept running out of fuel and ammo and was getting very frustrated so I read the instruction booklet and found that by shooting and destroying various buildings and objects I could pick up extra ammo and fuel and other things and win the game.

Nowadays with the Internet, there are various forums for just about everything. Try a Google search about your game and see what comes up. Some games even have strategy guides compiled about them. I recently purchased one for Juiced on the PS2. It contained maps of the circuits in both directions and details about the cars, various tips etc. *Draw or recreate the circuits to help your memory. Stick them on a wall if it helps. Professional racing drivers walk or drive the circuit before they race it!*

Know your controller, or joystick.

An analogue controller is vital for any serious gamer. When I got my PS1 it came with two normal controllers. These were plain compared to the analogue controllers which offer finer controls and even have vibration. Having the best stick or controller might not necessarily help you win the game though.

Don't get caught out not knowing which button to push to give you some extra turbo boost at the last minute. Make a map and or recreate the control guide for your instructions. Highlight the important buttons in different colours. Indeed, do the same if it's a keyboard game on a PC. Tom Clancy's Rainbow Six is a good example a game where lots of keys are used.

Editors and Games utilities.

Now I don't condone cheating in the real world. But sometimes when all else fails using a cheat utility may help you. I prefer to call this "Experimental Gaming".

These can come in the hardware or software format.

I remember the early cheat utilities that I bought. The first was the Freeze Machine (By Evesham Micros). It was a cartridge that was plugged into the back of the C64. It (hence it's name) had a freeze button that froze the game and allowed you to do all sorts of wonderful things like give yourself extra lives, ammo etc and generally become immortal. The cartridge had a built in reset switch which freed up a serial port. The next was the Datel Action Replay, again similar in design but with an extra software disk that allowed you to do more.

It was the highlight of the week when Zap 64 magazine to arrive at the newsagents and reading the cheats section. You had to freeze the game, then enter code in the form of poke commands to become invincible.

Datel are still going strong and produce an Action Replay disk for consoles. With this you can give yourself maximum money and a whole host of other cheats to enhance your gaming experience.

Sometimes you have to test a game to its limits to become master of it!

Some simulators and strategy games have editors that you either buy separately or come with the game. The first editor I purchased was a PD (Public Domain) software, very cheap for the game Microprose Grand Prix (Amiga). You could change the colours of the cars and create your own helmet and even team. The next one I brought was for Football Manager, again on the Amiga. I set about creating the perfect Liverpool. I changed the club's finances so they were the richest. I increased the stadium size so the club got richer with more ticket sales and added the best players of the time and gave them maximum wages. Who would have thought that Ryan Giggs would have played for Liverpool?? I was manager of the month for the whole season, we won every game and title. I still had to decide on the formation of the team and the strategy but it was great fun............

I'm doing the same with Football Manager 2008. I have Michael Owen, David Beckham, Wayne Rooney, Frank Lampard, etc, etc, all in the same team (see later).

I know I'm going on a bit but I'm just trying to show you what is possible with a little imagination.

So to refresh some main points.

1. Your memory is an asset, use it wisely.
2. The computer will run the same program over and over again.
3. Read your game manual or instruction booklet thoroughly.
4. Know your controller or Joystick.
Experiment with cheat utilities or editors.

Game types.

I'm going to start with film/movie and television tie in games.

In the 1980's a brilliant film called Ghost Busters was made. Not long after the computer game followed. Of course everyone who had a computer who had seen the film wanted the game including me. I had a games afternoon one Sunday with several friends and we were struggling with Ghost Busters, we lost time and time again. Our goal was first of all to buy the cheapest equipment because the game gave a limited budget then bust as many ghosts and eventually reach the Temple of Zuul and close a portal between the city and the spirit world. One friend suggested using the stream to drag the ghost to the area where the trap was.

"That's what they did in the film." he said smiling.

We tried and were successful 99.9% of the time. Our money built up and eventually we slipped past the marshmallow man and closed the portal.

This was vitally important as we got a bank account number and we would be able to start the game with our final money amount and be able to buy better equipment so we could complete the next game easier.

So if you are playing such a game always relate to the movie.

Arcade games and "Shoot em ups".

Never pass a chance to get extra lives, this might mean the difference between completing the game or having to try again. Some games have you complete a level before giving you an extra life, others have objects that you must collect or pick up before being rewarded. You can never have enough ammo, stockpile as much as you can. Memorize the places where you find them so you will get to them quicker. Most games nowadays have a pause button. Why not make a map and mark off which objects are where.

Racing Car Simulators.

These are my personal favourites.

Firstly, it would be impossible for me to tell you how to set up every racing car for every racing game. So, I am merely going to point you in the right direction for setting them up.

We will use Formula One cars as an example. Do not bother with manual gears, to begin with - this is where most fail, select auto gears and let the computer do the work for you. The only racing game I raced with manual gears was the Sega F1 game – I knew all the circuits like the back of my hands and the performance of the car improved.

The booklet that comes with Gran Turismo 4 (PS1) is a gold mine of information, almost a guide to setting up motor racing cars in itself.

Using a steering wheel and foot pedals:- personally, I prefer the hand held controller as I have been so used to using these. I tried a McLaren steering wheel and foot pedals on a PS1 but did not get on with it and reverted to the hand held controller. I get on fine on the full arcade machines though.

As with everything don't rush in. Setting up a car to your liking takes time and practice, that's why Formula One teams spend millions of pounds on testing each year.

Most of the Formula One games have a testing or practice option, so select this and choose a track. Monza, Italy is a great track, long straights and some chicanes to keep you on your toes.

From the setup menu, note down your settings, for tyre type, if using manual gears, you will need to set gear ratios. Set your brake balance, car balance, and finally rear wing setting.

Note them down, then exit the garage and take your car for a spin. F1 used to have a three lap qualifying session, which meant you would go out for a warm up lap, then do a flying lap and a cool down lap and come in for more tyres and now fuel.

The rules in F1 change every year, so I'm not going into this, just check your game booklet for the rules and objectives.

Start slowly, no hurry - you are testing...... Build up speed gradually, try to keep the car on the tarmac and pick out your breaking points, signs on the circuit, a bridge, etc.

The computer simulates tyre wear when you run off track (you get less grip). Likewise damage; if you hit another car, a wall, a barrier then your car will not feel the same after impact, this will cost you time, positions and points in a championship campaign.

Once on track, look for your on screen map – most gamers are too busy trying to stop themselves from flying off the track to notice this, but it is important – it is usually located to the left of the screen and your car is indicated by a coloured dot that gives you your position and other dots (usually white) that tell you where your competitors are on the track. If you get lost, forget where the pits are you will need this. Juiced and Juiced 2 Hot City Nights are excellent examples of racing games with an on screen map. The on screen maps have helped me to win on more than one occasion. I can see where I am on a circuit, who is close to me and who might be a danger to my position and compromise my victory.

Setting up a car used to be fairly straightforward, but with each New Year the game programmes improve. The rules change and more gadgets are put on the cars, they need more set up time. I will give a general idea but you need to check your game manual.

In the Sega F1 game, you had three things to set. Tyres, wing setting and gearbox.

My ideal Monza, setup:

Low wing setting, soft tyres (more grip but wear out faster), automatic transmission.

Let's start with wing settings.

A high wing setting gives more grip and glues the car to the track, but also reduces the speed of the car.

A low wing setting gives less grip and more speed. A medium wing setting is obviously in between the high and low setting.

Try to set the car up to your liking, don't be afraid to experiment with different settings.

Once you get practiced and comfortable you can switch to manual gears for the ultimate racing experience.

Tyre types.

You choose between the softer compound (more grip but wears out quicker), hard compound (less grip but lasts longer) and wet weather tyres.

Pit stops.

The timing of these is important. You will gain a feel of when the tyres are wearing, or if you have run off track a lot. Watch some Formula One races to see when the teams pit on certain tracks.

Usually it is two stops, but sometimes on longer race distances it is three.

I generally prefer shorter stints, rather than having to concentrate for longer laps.

Fuel Load.

If your game supports this then you can choose your fuel load. Depending on where you qualify, you must decide what amount to put in. If you qualify on pole position this is an advantage, providing you start well you can build up a reasonable gap from the cars behind you, pit when you have enough time to get back out in front or at the very least second. Don't rush into the pit lane, be calm and don't panic.

Have a clear idea before the start when you are going to pit, if necessary write down your fuel load before hand. A car with a light fuel load will be quicker than one with a heavy fuel load.

If you qualify last or mid field you may wish to carry a heavier fuel load and just pit for tyres.

Try and keep out of trouble at the start, avoid any collisions. One game, Toca Touring cars is a good example to quote. If you have had a collision with someone, the game was programmed to remember which driver you hit and then to allow the simulated driver to retaliate.

For a five lap race with fuel, if I was in pole I would aim to build up a healthy gap and pit by lap three, quick refill and tyre change, then be out in front again or at the very least second and with time to catch the leader and overtake.

On F1 97 (PS1), on long distance races I used to find the other cars would slow down towards the end of the race.

Two scenarios:-

You qualify in last position, a five lap race with the fuel option turned on.

Fill your car for five laps and the harder compound tyres. Try and make up as many places as you can at the start. Keep an eye on the others and avoid any contact. If you get into the lead then all well and good, but say you end up second or third, keep up with the leaders, stay off the grass and by lap three you will find the leaders will pit and if you have done everything right you will fly past them in the pits and be in the lead. Watch your tyres and if anyone catches you, keep your racing line for two laps and defend your position. You may need to pit, but just for a fresh set of tyres, you will also get quicker as your fuel load gets lighter.

With the weather set to variable. You qualify in pole position, try and build up a good lead. It will rain at the same point in each race. Be aware when you see spots of rain or the clouds darkening. Don't leave it too late to pit. Of course it might be a short shower which you might be able to get away with by staying out on your normal tyres. However, you will lose handling and grip. You will have to weigh up the options as to whether you can control the car for the remaining laps, or risk having an accident, spinning off the track and other cars on wet weather tyres will catch you. A tip – use manual gears to give more control, you can shift up and down a gear rather than the automatic transmission doing it for you.

Today, when the conditions get too much, a safety car is deployed, this gives the drivers time to pit for fresh tyres and fuel if required.

The Racing line – The Racing Line is the ideal route round any circuit. As the F1 cars lay down rubber from their tyres this line gets blacker and helps give more grip. Deviate from this line and you end up catching the "marbles" on the edge of the track, this can throw you off line and ruin your lap and or a race.

### First person shooters (FPS).

As a general rule, pick up any ammo and weapons that are lying around, you can never have too much ammo. However, it maybe worth leaving the odd bit of ammo around just in case you run out, so you can double back and recharge levels. Also discard any weapons that have run out of ammo, do not hang on to them if they cannot be reloaded with ammo or recharged. In one Pierce Brosnan James Bond film, Bond was in a battle and the machine gun ran out, Bond just chucked it away and moved on. I'm not saying I would have done the same thing, as I may have had the chance or the need to knock an enemy out with the butt of the gun.

As games get ever more realistic, be aware that if you are carrying something that isn't much use and there is a time limit to complete a stage, that non essential item may slow you down.

Shoot targets that are close to you or pose the most threat to you first. If a target starts shooting rockets at you that can cause damage and loss of a life, try and shoot the rocket and/or rockets that are being fired at you. This will save either your shield power or damage levels that eventually, when they reach critical, will result in loss of a life and your chance of progressing further in a game.

Look for first aid boxes or health boosters and pick them up where possible. Leave some in strategic places in case you need to back track to a certain point.

Some games repair shields or health levels when a specific score is reached, so be aware of when that time is.

Strategy Simulations (Including war games).

There is such a vast selection of strategy and war games out there that I will generalize what has worked for me in the past.

One of my favourite games in this genre is the original Age of Empires from Microsoft.

You need to start a civilization. In order to do this you need people, people need food and houses, this costs money and of course as your civilization grows other tribes make be looking for trouble unless you either trade with them and make allies or have enough armies both on land and sea to wipe out the opposition.

The way I play these games is to start small and build up gradually.

Set your first workers to gather wood and as soon as you can, build a port if it is a game based with sea involved. Build some fishing boats and look on the map to find the best area to fish. In a land based game you will need to use your villagers as hunters to hunt and kill the local animals and of course build farms to farm the land.

As your population grows you will need to build houses. Organise your workforce into groups. Builders, gold diggers, stone miners etc. The more you have the faster your stockpile will grow.

I should mention at this point that most games of this type will have a population limit, which when reached cannot be exceeded.

Try and build a market quickly and create either a scout or a scout ship.

As the game time moves forward settlements will appear on the map. Send a scout to your nearest rivals and establish a trading relationship.

As your funds grow, get your armed forces together. Place your garrison or garrisons in strategic places, near a port, or near wooded areas in cover. Also place watch towers around important buildings. They can also be an important line of first defence, to give you a chance to rally your troops.

There are many reasons another tribe may attack you and why you should decide to attack another tribe. One reason for an attack is that you have strayed on to another tribe's territory and begun taking gold from them or simply fishing or hunting in their territory.

If you get into an attack situation, don't take all your army. Leave some in case another tribe decides to attack you whilst you are away fighting.

I'm not going to go into a detailed guide of battle, just give you a few pointers.

Don't waste time moving one unit at a time, most games allow you to select multiple units using the mouse or a keyboard short cut.

For a sea based game. I would build several transport ships and load my troops/weapons on to them, then select my fleet and move them to the target area. I use the fleet as a distraction and land my ground troops with whatever weapons they have for that particular era. Divide your men, attack the watch towers or defences with one group. Also attack the villagers being aware that if there are any left they can rapidly rebuild/repair defences, ships, garrisons etc.

If you have enough units attack the fishing boats and food stores, a starving settlement cannot survive.

The thing I like about Age of Empires Gold Edition is that as you progress through the ages you get the chance to build different buildings such as temples where you can create priests or wizards who can work magic in your favour. Wizards are useful in this game because they can heal wounded, convert enemy soldiers or population to your side and convert buildings and weapons to your side.

I would generally have one or two wizards accompanying an attacking force. Beware though if the other side has wizards or priests they have the same power. They also get drained of energy depending on the size of the task you give them.

If your game has a recruit spy option, be careful where you send them, they may well come back as double agents.

## Sports Simulations.

The good old days of the Joystick breakers like Daly Thompson's Decathlon and Summer Games are well remembered.

Again know the rules and your controller. Keep a track of your score. Know how much you need to qualify for each event. You will soon know which events you are good at and which events you are not good at.

Remember the words in that song the late great Roy Castle used to sing "Dedication" If you want to be the best then dedication is what you need.

Good luck and happy winning.

You will find numerous cheat and tips sites on the world wide web, just Google search the game of your choice and many pages should appear.

Use the hints and walk through wisely. Look at the FAQ's sections on web sites, you may even find yourself chatting with someone from the other side of the world about your favourite games.

## Final Thoughts…………………………

## Game Preferences and Options.

Use these to customise your controller, sound and display settings. Set the controller or keys so that you can remember them easily.

I found with Rome Total War I had my own General as an adviser, he guided me through the first battle and taught me where to place my troops, etc. I could even turn him off if I wanted to. Use everything you can to your advantage.

If you have a Joystick with an auto fire switch, make sure it is turned off for games that do not require it!

How To <u>Really</u> Beat Computer Games - Part Two.

Burnout 2 is a good game to play without using any cheat codes. Once you get at least a bronze medal in the offensive driving 101 courses you will unlock other game modes.

Know and understand what the challenges are before you start the game. Scroll through the circuits to find out which races unlock other races and secret cars.

Read through the user manual and memorise the controls on your controller.

Car control and memory of the circuit you are racing on is important. There is nothing like the feeling of seeing perfect lap flash up. When you think you are going to crash and are in the lead, aim for long vehicles, lorries, busses, etc. Hitting these at junctions will cause multiple pile ups and still allow you restart in the lead. The more damage caused the more the insurance money builds up.

Choose from either a single race or championship, then select your car. I personally look for a car which has good control, that doesn't necessarily mean it has the best acceleration rate. It is good car control that will keep you ahead of the chasing pack. Now you need to select automatic or manual transmission. Again whilst learning the circuits I find automatic transmission useful.

At the start, waiting for the count down, push the accelerator button forward and keep the engine revs at maximum. You should be able to get away in the lead, maybe having to dart from left to right to defend your position. Just hitting a car alongside you is enough to make them back off. Use the L1 button to flick the screen to the rear view to see where you opponents are.

Keep an eye for the green direction signs and also watch when your indicator lights flashes either left or right.

Light up that Burn meter.

Using your offensive driving skill, by either drifting, doing near misses and driving on the wrong side of the road. Look out for dips in the road and drive over them at speed jumping into the air. A good pro tip is to keep the R1 button on through out game play. This saves you thinking about pushing it when the meter reaches maximum.

Use barriers to slow down, don't wallop them, just scrape and watch the sparks fly. Likewise with vehicles, a light tap won't do you any harm but a head on hit at a certain point will do.

When learning a circuit it is sometimes easier following a leading car, but you will need lightning reactions and have to be ready to move out of the way quickly as and when they crash. If you are chasing cars, try spooking them, that is tailgating them so that they get frustrated and either back off or crash. You will need to be reading the road ahead though. Spooking is a neat trick in multi player games.

Juiced is a good example of this. During a race there is a "Spook" bar, and when the bar reaches maximum the "spooked" driver pulls over. If you are aware that this is happening to you focus on the road ahead and try all avoiding actions you can find. No one likes being tail gated in the real world or the virtual world.

If you loose watch the replay to find out where you went wrong. Always remember the same cars and other vehicles will appear at exactly the same position on each circuit every time you play the game.

There have been one lap races where I have been dead last and almost given up hope only to see the pack I'm chasing up front have a multiple crash, then I've come through at the last minute to win.

So, never give up as the phrase goes "It isn't over till the fat lady sings.".

When in pursuit of the bad guys car, try to ram the target car as much as possible, try to push it into barriers and other vehicles. Watch the count down time and the damage indicator on screen to gage the condition of the target car. Once you get it smoking you know you are nearly on the road to success and the chase is over.

It is possible to save you burnout boost and keep the meter glowing so long as you don't crash.

Another good way of learning the circuits, is to video them whilst you are racing. Most digital cameras have a record option. Have a friend record you or record them whilst they are playing.

I have found the Burnout series of games great fun and very addictive. Please remember that it is just a game and please drive safely on the real roads.

More on Game Editors.

My first dabble into football management game editors happened with the Commodore Amiga 500. These editors are a fantasy football managers dream. Editors allow you to create your "dream team", and do all manner of things to make you the number one manager.

Where do you start though?

Select your favourite team, for me it's always either Liverpool or Man Utd. Then take a look at the finances. If possible adjust the stadium size to maximum, this will increase the number of seats and thus bring in more revenue from away supporters and home supporters. Next, I'll adjust the various ticket prices to maximum, again more revenue and the fans won't mind or complain because they're not real!

Now I'll try and get a maximum annual budget - billions of pounds is what's needed. On Football Masters for the Amiga by ESP this was easy - unlimited funds, but it took a bit of doing in Sega's FM 2008. Now it's time to look over your squad.

FM 2008 editor is superb. You can adjust the height, weight, race and skill levels of each player. With regards to players wages I will always adjust their weekly amount to maximum - my mode of thinking is, Ryan Giggs on three million pounds a week is more likely to score more goals than Ryan Giggs on one hundred pounds per week. Of course with the right squad selection you don't have to select that player each week.

To give an example of editing a team, a good defence would be four well built coloured players. Another example is after searching the list of players, I found Robbie Fowler and adjusted his age to seventeen. Also have a tall player in your squad with good heading skills, well placed when a corner is taken they can invaluable. Peter Crouch is an example of a player that would not need his height adjusting. Some editors will allow you to change whether the player is left of right footed.

I now find myself thinking like an England coach and searching my memory of the best players in Europe and the Premiership and around the world. As the FA have now introduced transfer windows it's far better to select your "dream squad" at the beginning.

For example, my dream Liverpool would include the following players:- Rooney, Ronaldo, Giggs, Beckham, Terry, Ferdinand, Lampard, Gerrard, Torres, etc. I would also select and edit enough back up players to be playing them on a rotation system, or in the reserve squad.

Another thing to think about is the various competitions, be careful to have a squad were certain players don't get cup tied or are ineligible to play.

FM 2008's editor allows you to select an option where the player doesn't get injured or has a reduced injury risk.

Tactics and game play.

Editors alas, will not allow you to change the rules of the game. Pay attention to what your scouts say and look at the formations the other teams use. If you intend to play games at a high tempo then be aware that your "dream team" players will get tired and may not perform or train to their best ability. I found that playing two high tempo games per week and maximum training really wears players out, and don't forget the Prima Donna who asks for time off for personal reasons when you least expect it.

If you have set high skills levels for each squad member then you need to leave the training on low and perhaps award the players a day off on Monday to recover, or a day off after an important game. I have found that starting a game with a high tempo produces goals, then reducing the pace a little and being defensive actually wins the game. Of course you can have too slow a pace and be too defensive and your give your opponents a chance to slip the ball into the back of the net when you were least expecting it.

Sometimes you will be able to play a 4-5-1 system if you have a striker on form. Other games you will have to use a 4-4-2 or even a 4-3-3. Experiment with the formations - you may be surprised.

Substitutes - This can be a nightmare. Domestic competitions require you have four substitutes, other competitions you can have as many as six.

Personally, I always try to have one sub from each department so to speak, that is goal, defence, midfield and attack. When to change, is the sixty four thousand dollar question. You must judge each players performance on the pitch. Sometimes a change at half time can inject a fresh pace, other times leaving a change late in the game when your are winning can delay proceedings (time wasting in effect, but without a player being penalised). I have found on FM 2008 that even with the reduced injuries option selected players can get injured, striker's and midfielder's seem especially prone.

FM 2008 is excellent in giving you data on a players performance levels. Check the percentage levels, they will soon tell you if they are feeling excellent or tired during a game. 100% is top fitness level. I personally worry when the percentage starts dropping. I never keep a player on with less than fifty percent as their is risk of injury or mistakes being made - you will also have to rest the player the following day or even for several days. Of course if you are out of options then you have no choice but to keep that player on for the remainder of the game.

Another tip is not to have your goal keeper stray too far from his box when kicking the ball up field. When I was manager of Chelsea the goal keeper was a pain to get to stay back, and as a result my opponents striker's scored several easy goals with an open opportunity.

My advice is to keep a journal. Jot down your tactics and the formations of your opponents and also scores, baring in mind that the simulation runs the same way each time.

I like the Sega game engine for their Football Manager games. The way you can pair members of your squad with each other, for example a senior member paired with a junior member of the team to learn from them. Also, the admin side has been well thought through even down to an inbox for emails.

There is however, a down side to using editors. I had created what I thought to be the perfect Liverpool squad. I won every single game and the premiership using clever squad rotation and using the best players in the world, been manager of the month on numerous occasions, had a Man City style budget. When I reached the European cup final and was winning the game, it just froze on me after a certain player scored a number of goals. I tried restarting the simulation, but the same thing happened repeatedly. On talking to various people, this apparently is not uncommon. I can only assume that there is a line of code inserted at a certain point in the programme that prevents you from winning everything.

Thinking about it, the games creators would not want you to easily be winning everything as you would soon get fed up with playing the game and move onto another one.

I can't comment on network or multi manager playing, as I have only pitted my wits against the computer simulation. The obvious thing is that you will be playing against a human with intelligence, rather than just a computer running lines of instruction code over and over again.

As already mentioned if your game has an advisor, turn it on if you are just starting out and follow it's advice (You can always turn it off when you don't need it). Also study the manual - FM 2008's manual is some 55 pages long and full of useful tips. Already a football fan, I found it useful to watch matches and make mental notes on the various strategies and team formations that managers would implement. It is also useful to listen to the various football pundits comments, especially the ex players, they more often than not, know what they are talking about!

## Notes for beating Facebook and other Internet computer games.

The trouble with Internet games like Mafia Wars, Rock Legends, etc created by Zynga, is that they rely on impatient people who wish to spend money to increase their health, energy and stamina levels, either by using Pay Pal or Amazon payments and the many other sponsored companies who will gift you reward points after you either make a purchase or fill out a survey. These reward points can be used to increase Health, Energy, Stamina and even street credit. There is no need to spend money, but some people will just go all out to win the game, when all you need is a little patience.

My first tip is to find the free reward points offers and yes I know it's a pain, but it's worth filling out a survey or two to get some free reward points.

Any newbie to Mafia Wars gets 100/100 Health – 10/10 Energy – 3/3 Stamina, 11 Godfather points and +5 profile points and $8,000 to spend.

Please, please, do not rush out and spend the Godfather reward points straight away, keep them as backup, likewise the free +5 profile points – it's tempting to increase your Energy levels straight away, but just wait and have patience until you reach level 2. I have noticed that when you complete a level your Health, Energy and Stamina are recharged to maximum as a bonus.

Always divide your reward points equally between Health, Energy and Stamina. Try not to have one running away too much ahead. The Stamina is a problem as it always costs 2 reward points to top up.

Example:-

I am at level 3, having 11 Godfather points and +10 profile points – keep checking your experience points to find out when you next complete a level and get the next +5 profile points. Start gradually increasing your Health, Energy and Stamina, hereby known as H.E.S. Always keep some reward points in reserve just in case.

Jobs.

I do jobs in a methodical manner, starting from the top of the list and working down, as H.E.S allows and recharges. Once your energy reduces to a zero, you will not be able to do the mainstream jobs which earn you experience points and cash. Also look for the Loot jobs, these will give you Health Kits and other useful items. I read somewhere recently that a player should save their energy until such a time that it is at maximum level and concentrate on doing the jobs that receive the most points towards completing a level. This is not always the case. As someone starting out, you will have to do the jobs which pay out less experience points to get some money to purchase the items required to do the bigger pay out jobs. There will also come a time in each job where you can earn a job bonus and get help from your crew. What else can I do?

Whilst you wait for your energy to recharge you can always look at either attacking (fight) other mafia or even robbing and doing hit list jobs, robbing will eat your health and stamina, your energy level remains the same. I find it best to sucker punch someone quite a few times, before taking your mafia on a full scale attack (this will reduce your stamina). Always examine your targets Mafia size, weapons, armour and vehicles. It's unwise to try and take on someone with a Mafia size greater than your own on a first attempt, unless you are going to sucker punch them a lot.

If you intend on robbing someone frequently be aware that they may return the favour depending on how often they play Mafia Wars, make sure you keep your property health and protection status at full. I never leave much money lying around for any one to steal from me. Wait until you have say 2 or 3 thousand dollars then put it straight in the bank, it's worth paying the 10% laundering fee, rather than someone else having it. Also, make sure your property is fully protected.

Unfortunately, people with larger Mafia or Crew size will always attack and rob the little guys and cost you money in both property protection and health. However, if you have done your recruiting job properly you should be able to be the one picking on the little guys.

13/8/09 tip, I was playing Mafia Wars today and found "Default Don" on the list of Mafia for fighting, not sure if this is a test by the game creators, but he only had 32 Mafia members and was an easy target!

Businesses. I find that once you start recruiting your Mafia via your on line friends and other methods, start buying as many abandoned lots and Mafia Mikes, this should be enough to provide a good income. Remember deposit money in the bank regularly, withdrawing is free. You also complete an achievement award on depositing $1,000,000.

I should mention also, that if you are fighting etc. you should keep some money available to recharge your health at the very expensive hospital.

## Cuba level tip 35

When you first arrive in Cuba, earning money is a tough business. It is slow and uses your energy. If you end up fighting or being attacked, do not spend your Cuban pesos on restoring your health, fly straight back to New York and use any income or savings from your efforts there to heal yourself in New York.

I saved hard for the first business in Cuba which is the Bodega, producing canned goods. I used the money from this to buy weapons, local thugs and local guides. When I had enough of these I was able to do the bigger payout jobs and therefore upgrade the business to more capacity and output, thus bringing more money.

Growing your Mafia –

To grow your Mafia – how dedicated a player are you?

The first port of call should be like minded friends and family.

It is simply amazing how many people from my school days I have found on Facebook and it is very easy to build up a network. Friends will tell their friends and so and so fourth.

These friends/family members can be valuable assets and gift you items when you most need them.

I also recommend putting your recruiting link for any of the games on the various forums and mailings lists elsewhere on the Internet. Also use Bee Boo, My Space and Twitter. This can produce a lot of traffic on your wall/time line though. Also, do join the various forums on Facebook and read the emails they send.

Please add the title of your game/application in your recruiting link e.g. "Mafia Wars" please come and join my gang etc. There are a lot of children out there playing these games, so please make sure you let anyone wanting to join your crew and be friends with you, what you are planning!

If you are still at school, college or university ask your friends there, you could put a notice on any notice boards. Are you at work? Try recruiting your colleagues, but do ask your boss first if it is all right to do so and do not use work time to play games, unless it is your lunch hour of course – I'm sure any boss would agree with me!!

There are many, many blogs out there, you could search for gaming blogs and 'Guest Post' or even start your own blog describing your gaming adventures, you never know, you might build yourself a following or fan base.

Keep your income higher than you outgoings, i.e. be patient enough to get businesses first that will bring you top $ in return and then start buying the land, weapons (get as many Chain Guns as money permits) etc. Always start with the smaller jobs energy wise and build some cash. If you have too much upkeep and deposit in the bank, they will take your deposit to pay for your upkeep

In Pirates Rule the Caribbean, do the simple jobs and build your income enough to get you through to level two, then start working logically through each job, purchasing the necessary weapons and gaining enough money toward purchasing a pirate islands, under the properties link - the frozen island costs 22,400, but your returns will be like owning Mafia Mikes in Mafia Wars. Do not over spend on weapons, vehicles etc until you have enough cash flow, otherwise any money you have left over will be robbed by another gamer or if you stashed it in the bank minus that 10% deposit fee will be withdrawn without your permission to pay the upkeep of your inventory.

Note, Purchasing Frozen Islands requires you to recruit more members to your crew, once you reach a certain number.

Simple – More Income pays for upkeep of both properties and weapons/vehicles/armour. Keep yourself on the + side all the time.

What I like about Pirates Rule the Caribbean, is that you can top up your energy levels by visiting the Home page and with just a few mouse clicks you can top up your energy. This is useful at the end of a days play to feed your pet and keep it's well being and happiness up to full levels.

Gifting – I always return the favour when someone sends me a gift. In some games, this is a great way to get some free items to start making some cash without visiting which ever GM or Game Boss is in charge of the game (Davey Jones, The Godfather etc.). FarmVille is a good example, where in earlier levels there is a good selection of trees, that when fully grown, you can harvest them and get some much needed cash.

It's great when someone comes aboard your crew and sends you an energy pack, these people are like gold dust, nurture them and keep them sweet. Always send energy, etc back to your crew and keep an eye on when the next pack will be available, it could mean the difference between completing a level or not!

Bragging. Most of these games give you the chance to brag on your wall, which will be viewable by your friends. Personally I don't do this too often, just occasionally, when appropriate. Whilst it's nice to shout about your success, peoples walls get so much clutter that they probably wont even notice.

This article deals with the Facebook game FarmVille created or built by Zynga.

I am going to explain how to run your farm.

Each time you login to Facebook, you receive notifications for each application that you are using, friend requests, gift requests, etc. Go to your home page first and start collecting and accepting either gifts or requests first, you will automatically be asked if you have more pending gifts for whichever application you are using.

You may have to sell the gifts your friends give you in the early stages to gain some coins or fill out a free survey to get some coins. Every day on your first playing you receive ten free coins, plus bonuses for certain achievements. Always gift back, using the free gift option. Don't send a gift from your own collection unless you can afford to lose one item. Both Farm Ville and Mafia Wars have the option to select your friends that are using that application, but there is a limit each time.

When starting out on Farm Ville, decide on how many plots of land you are going to have. Then use the plough (spelling this word the English way or plow as it is in Farm

Ville) tool to create a grid. I personally prefer a ten by ten plot when starting out.

This gives you the chance to plant several types of crop in each row:- one row of five raspberries, the next wheat, the next super berries, etc. As you progress through the levels you will unlock different crops that will give you more income in coins, likewise with buildings, animals and decorations. Don't forget to note down the grow time and return as and when appropriate to harvest your crops, whether it be two hours or three days for anything to be ready to harvest or collect.

I tend to do things in an organised manor. On any given visit to my Farm I will check first of all what crops are ready for harvesting. If none then I will check whatever animals are highlighted as being ready for collection of their eggs, milk, truffles, etc. Then I will move my mouse pointer over the trees to find out what (%) percentage their growth is, usually these having being gifted by friends who are playing the game, if they require harvesting then I will collect the coins in the process.

Next, I will visit my friends farms and do jobs for them on their farms. All "Help" jobs give you 20 coins and 5 experience, so do this as and when possible, the experience points always helping towards the next level. This is a great coins and experience points earner and not to be overlooked.

Harvesting alone, does not gain you experience points. Ploughing and planting crops does.

When you get a chance and have enough neighbours expand your farm, so you can reap the benefits with animals and produce.

Always have goals:- what do you expect to achieve from your farm. Do you wish to organise your animals by creating a nice white wash fence enclosure, purchase a red barn, or a tractor to speed up ploughing. Do the maths, using you desktop calculator or real world calculator, work out how much every action costs.

A quick return. When you plough one plot of fallow land, it costs fifteen coins and gains you one experience point. Next buy some Super Berries and plant those, they will be ready for harvesting in two hours, so don't forget to check back and collect your coins. You will receive 100 coins for the Berries and 1 experience point.

A tractor is an expensive luxury, but does making the ploughing quicker. Just as an example ploughing two plots of land costs 2 fuel, 30 coins gives you 2 experience points. The Tractor fuel recharges when you first visit your farm every so often.

Expanding your farm.

The ultimate goal is to be able to expand your farm, so you can plough more plots and plant more seeds, keep more animals and earn more money. To do this you need to add your friends..

One other way of recruiting friends is to do a search for your old school friends. I typed in some names on the search option and sure enough, people who I knew some 20 years ago have accounts. I have rapidly expanded my

Mafia, in Mafia Wars by clicking on the Mutual friends links when Facebook make suggestions as to other people you may know. When I make contact with these people I always include a link to the game I am playing. I also have a photo on my wall so people may or may not recognise me. FarmVille and Mafia Wars allow you to select from a list of friends playing the same game. In Pirates Rule the Caribbean, you have to recruit them from your friend list.

So, you want to be a Pirate? Rule the seas, getting tons of gold and becoming famous or infamous?

Well, with Facebook and Zynga you can, so login and select Pirates: Rule the Caribbean from the list of applications and click allow application and off you go to lots of adventures.

Choose your pirate name, then select which type of character you are going to be:

Scallywag (gets gold faster).

Buccaneer (gains health faster)

Swashbuckler (gains energy faster)

Choose your character depending on how quickly you wish to obtain the gold, or your health or energy to recharge.

The screen will change and you'll receive a message saying you've earned 8 experience points for creating a character. You will receive a message saying Captain Wiggins is now in your crew. So now click on the start playing button and begin your adventure. Another message appears saying you have been given 3,000 gold.

Notice there is only one experience point to level 2.

Now you need to visit the crew page and start sending requests for friends to join you. Depending on how many reply and how quickly, you will soon be able to purchase a limited edition island and start making money.

Whilst you are waiting for your friends to join you, go to the mission page and do the first mission on the list "Count yer ill-gotten treasure." This will use one energy and give you between 30 and 80 gold (depending on how the programme runs) and give you one experience point towards getting to the next level and your gold will end up being approximately just around 3,045. Hang off buying that pet just yet and keep doing that mission until you complete it. Why, well you'll see in just a minute.

With 15 energy, you will complete the mission with 6 energy left and 2 experience points to level 3, plus 3,492. The reward varies every time you do the mission, but is always the same – remember the game follows a programme and never deviates from it.

Don't forget to "click on the earn a job bonus button" and get help from your crew. Always use this opportunity in any game.

So, now you have approx 3,492 gold, there are a few options to consider:-

1. You would like to do the next mission on the list which gives you 2 experience points and requires the purchase of a Stick o' Wood. This gives you one attack, 0 defence and costs 300 gold, with zero upkeep.

2.  You would like to purchase a pet to help you on missions or aid you in fights.

Personally, I would visit Davey Jones and use 10 of my "favor" points to receive 10,000 gold. That gives you approx 13,492 gold to spend. Your friends have now joined your crew and you go ahead and purchase a Rum Island or whichever limited edition property (these change frequently, so check how many crew members you require) is available. You will receive your income in 54 minutes of 12,000.

You can now purchase a pet and set up a free island and hired three friends to collect, wood, stone, etc. This you can use to trade or buy buildings with. Don't let it decay otherwise you will have to clean it up.

Add territories and operations as and when the income allows. You unlock more at certain levels.

Now purchase a Stick o' wood and a dagger. The Stick o wood costs 300 gold and has zero upkeep and the dagger costs 700 gold and has zero upkeep. Add weapons and crafts as and when necessary.

The above is just one strategy, bear in mind that the limited edition properties are like Mafia Mikes in Mafia Wars. Of course you could always buy gold or fill out some free surveys for more "Favor" Points.

Now you've got some income going and have started your adventures, lets explain the main page and the various options.

When you start the game you are presented with a page that you can use to navigate to various tasks etc. Home, Missions, Fight, Armoury (U.S spelling armory), Properties, Island, Crew, Visit Davey Jones. You can also check for updates, find out who is infamous and access help.

Let's explain what happens when you click on each of these links.

Home.

The home page is where you go to find out the status of your island, the energy level happiness of your pet, crack locks in Poseidon's chest, do crew actions, send energy to your crew, buy special items, visit Davey Jones. You can also check your updates to find out when you were last attacked. Also on this page you can access sign up to twitter and install the Pirates tool bar to your browser and earn free favor Points

There is also a main menu, with links to the above and also Bounties, Treasure Chest, Loot Items, Me Crew, Most Infamous and Pirate Islands.

You can sign up to the Pirates mailing list from this page. There is a delete option to allow you to remove any updates that you do not wish to see.

Also on each page you Gold, Health, Energy, Strength, Experience, level are displayed.

Expert Tip:-

**Don't waste your free favor points at the beginning of a new game. Just as an example:- You have ten "favor" points free to begin with, rather than rush and recharge your energy, go to Davey Jones and find the Davey Jones offers ye 10,000, click on this and your money will be delivered straight away. Assuming you have done your recruiting well, now go to the properties page and look for the limited Edition Property, this used to be a Frozen Island, but these have now sold out. Luckily the income stays the same, but the cost of the limited edition property varies. Your gold income comes in every 54 minutes.**

## Missions.

This is the jobbing part of Pirates, where you gain experience points towards completing the level and progressing through the game. In the early stages, when you energy is low, you will have to do the missions that pay out fewer experience points. First look what weapons or items are needed in order to complete the mission, then purchase them in the armoury. Keep your pet energy levels topped up. You can pet it which is free but getting full happiness will reduce your energy.

Look for loot missions, which give you special items that you cannot buy. Look for the green rumoured to loot statement.

### Expert Tip:-

**Don't waste your energy on topping up your pets happiness and energy. Go to the home page and start doing crew actions by clicking on the do it button, the more crew you have the more you can recharge you**

**energy. Another good idea is to wait until your energy is at maximum before you do this. Also look out for when someone has sent you energy and always send energy to your crew.**

Fight.

When you click on the fight button you are shown a list of other pirates. Their names are displayed, as is their levels and crew sizes. Don't try and attack someone with a bigger crew size than your own. Also you can sword fight and place bounties on any one who you feel has been attacking you too much. There is also the brothel to visit for a massage after a hard days fighting.

Armoury (U.S spelling Armory).

As the name suggests, this is where you purchase you weapons, vessels, etc. Look at the defence/attack rating and also check for upkeep costs. Different items are unlocked at certain levels, so you will be able to chose from offensive, defensive and movement items.

Properties.

We have covered the limited edition properties. Here you can add anything from a secret cave to a dock and also a tariff station. Look at what you need to purchase first, for example a treasure stash consumes a secret cove.

Island.

From the Island button, you can access resources, buildings, trading post and crew islands. Click on the resources button and you are given the option to hire friends to collect wood, stone and iron. As these are stockpiled you can use the wood, etc. to build buildings. Certain buildings give you an energy boost or an attack advantage or a discount on defensive items.

When you've done building you can also trade your resources for gold, health refills, or energy boost, there is also a random loot offer.

By accessing your crews' islands, you can either steal or help out. Personally, I don't like the help out option on this game. There is every chance your friends may not return the favour. Whereas in FarmVille, when you visit/help out a friend you are given 20 coins and 5 experience points, there is no immediate reward in Pirates, until your friends decide they will help you out.

You can steal friends resources for a bit of fun, but they will likely return the favour and even kick you off their crew list, it does cost 1,000 coins to remove a crew member.

Crew.

The number of crew is shown in brackets. From this page you can send requests and add top mates, you can also send energy, once every 24 hours.

Me Stats.

This is where you can use your skill points, to increase energy and health levels, etc.

You will find you can check your pet's level, energy and happiness and top the latter up. There is a list of jobs completed, fights won, fights lost. Also you'll find your island status, your "Booty" income and upkeep. List of weapons both defensive and offensive, transport and territory owned.

You can also post a comment to your crew members which is free or for a non member 1,000 gold.

There is also a link to Poseidon's chest so you can go and crack locks.

Things to bear in mind.

Always keep your income higher than your upkeep or outgoings. Your health, energy and stamina are recharged when you complete each level. So keep your skill points until your complete a level and then use them. You are also given a skill point on completing a mission, save this until you complete a level.

Also remember, the higher your health, if you are attacked or indeed fight the more it is going to cost you in the brothel. Never leave much money lying around, someone will only come and attack you and you'll lose it. Bury it for a rainy day!

If only real life was like this I would be laughing (pirate style) all the way to the bank.

## How To Get The Most From Facebook

Facebook and other Internet social networking web sites have exploded in popularity over the last few years. Whole families have signed up with accounts in order to keep in touch, find new friends and use the variety of applications that are available.

There are many advantages and some pitfalls, people will always try and abuse such sites. I am going to explain how to get the best from using your Facebook account.

First of all, you need to decide what you expect to gain from these sites. Do you wish to play games and have fun with the multitude of applications that spring up so frequently that it is often difficult to keep track of.

When Facebook introduced the wall, any comments you share and that of your friends appear on every friend's wall in your network. Recently I was told someone had created a photo and actually allowed the application access. It turned out that someone had taken bits from various photo's and put them all on one. It was supposed to be funny, but wasn't really and provoked quite an angry response including swear words from someone in my network. You can easily hide any threads that are posted on your wall, but that is permanent. Please keep your language respectful. Another thing that seemed to happen a lot was I would be playing an application like FarmVille or Mafia Wars and I would get a message flashed up saying 5 of your friends in Manchester think your are stupid or similar. I was curious as I don't know anyone who lives in Manchester so I clicked on the link and got a screen asking me to enter my mobile number in order to find out who was thinking I was stupid. Well, I'm not that stupid and came off that site and stopped playing the application for a while, they seem to have stopped.

So, are you going to have a photo or not?

Some people are too embarrassed to have a photo of themselves. However, how do you expect people who may want to keep in touch with you to know what you look like? As a pianist I use Facebook primarily to promote the albums that I have recorded, so for me a photo is essential. So that anyone wishing to join my network knows it is John Clare the piano teacher/tuner/pianist/author and not John Clare living in Canada or somewhere else. I have seen pictures of peoples cats or other favourite animals and also cartoon characters though.

There is the option to include an album of photo's and also video. This can be good if you have attended a friend or relatives birthday party or even a sporting event.

I went to see Ken Dodd in Blackpool (a joint Birthday present between my Father and I for my Mother). It was five hours of comedy and entertainment. Fortunately, I didn't have any work the following day, was feeling slightly worse for wear, so took a collection of photo's and posted them just for a laugh.

You can use your digital camera or even web camera to take photo's. Adjust them to the correct size using MGI photo suite or whatever manipulation software came with your product.

Fill out your profile, listing your location and your date of birth (this makes it easier for people to find you). Then it's up to you whether you list your interests or not.

<u>Finding your friends.</u>

One way is to start typing their names into the search option box. This can prove tricky as not everyone has a photo and their current location listed. The best way I have found is by typing in friends whom I knew at school. People seem only to happy to increase their network size. Once you start adding people you know, when you login to Face Book they will list mutual friends, so you can send requests and then they can confirm they knew or know you.

Another example:- I lived in the same town for 27 years until finally my parents semi retired and we moved up North. I typed in some names of my students and people who lived in the same road as me and sure enough they had Facebook accounts. This opened up more people from their Network of friends.

As someone who is promoting their music on this site, this is invaluable as Reverb Nation created an application that allows some of my tunes and also a "you tube" video to appear on my profile. This is great, 10 people hear my tunes and like them, then recommend another ten of their friends and the money starts rolling in.

<u>Games and Applications.</u>

At the time of writing, you can be anything from a Mafia boss to a Pirate who Rules the Caribbean to a simple farmer. You can also work as a secret agent, run your own racing team and play Texas Poker. If you've never lived in a city, then you can experience city living with your friends without the expense of moving.

People do get carried away. I could quite easily waste an entire day on Facebook. The games are easily addictive, so you will have to be self disciplined. I only now have three main games which I play on a regular basis. I do use other games but not on a regular basis, I simply wouldn't get any work done.

Decide what you like, not every game appeals to everyone. Although when you see adverts saying fourteen million players yesterday it is very tempting to launch forth the application and click the allow button.

The problem with these games is that Zynga the games creator did not build any cheats in to the programmes. There is a reason for this:- they wish you to purchase coins or reward points in order to be able to progress through the levels of the game, this makes them richer. They also offer you the chance to gain reward points or coins by visiting one of their sponsors and either filling out a survey or purchasing something, usually some credit with a gambling game. Always look for the no purchase necessary offers, you will have to fill out a form with personal information and on completion your coins will be sent.

Don't waste your free "Favor" points at the beginning of new game. Just as an example:- I started playing Pirates: Rule the Caribbean. You have ten "favor" points free to begin with, rather than rush and recharge your energy go to Davey Jones and find the Davey Jones offers yer 10,000 click on this and your money will be delivered straight away. Assuming you have done your recruiting well, now go to the properties page and look for a limited Edition sitting on a beach even! If you are not fortunate to posses any of the above technology then you will find yourself losing your income, etc. from games. You can always ask a trusted friend to take over the playing for you, they will need your Email address and password to be able to login - problem sorted, discuss your strategies and hopefully you will come back to a thriving empire.

If none of the above is possible, then my advice is to bury or deposit any money. If you have recurring income then it will just mount up until you return. Depending on how often you are attacked your health will diminish as will your stamina. Your stamina will recharge over time, but on your return your will have to visit the doctor or whatever healing service is available and pay to recharge your health level.

On-line Chat.

This is a great chance to catch up with your friends. I was playing FarmVille one morning when someone I was at college with nearly 20 years ago started chatting with me about people we both knew and where they may or may not be nowadays. Locate the chat box when you login and notice how many of your friends are On line, you can then select anyone in particular and have a private chat with them.

Conclusion.

This has been an enjoyable article to write. As more and more info is published on the internet, more businesses will be creating applications for interaction with these sites. I guess we already have people who totally rely on these sites, a 24/7 community where you can contact anyone at all times of the day and night. What may happen in the future though? Will the bubble burst like it does with so many ideas? Or will these sites be a permanent feature of our lives?

Of course there is a negative side, and that is when an application is down or undergoing maintenance. There are also busy times when the net seems to get clogged up due to the number of people using it. These are usually peak times, evenings, weekends and public holidays. There is some lag, this being when you try and do something and there is no response for a certain amount of time. For example, you could be clicking on an animal in FarmVille to collect some milk or whatever and nothing happens for a bit. I guess as processor and server speed increase, lag will hopefully eventually be a thing of the past.

Getting into the "Gamers Zone"

The reader may have heard the term the "Zone" referred to by sports people and musicians alike. The "Zone" is where mind and body appear to be working at one and everything from a perfect serve, a superbly taken penalty or even the best of qualifying laps for a Grand Prix comes together.

In any game there is a conflict of your inner self. In Timothy Gallwey's book The Inner Game Of Tennis, he says that within each player there are two "Selves". Self 1 and Self 2.

Self 1 is the teller, while Self 2 is the doer. So imagine a game situation where you are just about to start a motor race. Let's use as an example the street racing game Need For Speed Nitro.

You are starting a circuit race in eighth position, using a Nintendo Wii controller with Nunchuck attachment.

Self 1 is telling you to keep pushing the A button to keep revving the engine in the green zone as the count down begins from 3 to 1, after 1, Self 1 now tells you to push the A button to launch the car and begin chasing the others until you reach first place and hopefully win the race.

During game play, Self 1 will instruct Self 2 which buttons to press to control the car, which pickups to collect and when to use your Nitro boost. If Self 1 is doing it's job correctly it is also thinking about other game objectives and picking up style points to earn you stars, etc.

When I was growing up, it was the hey day of what we now term vintage computers, the Sinclair ZX Spectrum and Commodore 64 to name but a few were very popular. Each week magazines would come out for the various manufacturers. The magazines contained reviews for up and coming games, cheat codes and more importantly maps or screen shots of some games, showing where extra lives/ammo, etc were located.

With digital cameras improving constantly, you no longer have to wait several weeks to receive your printed photographs. You can use this to your advantage by snapping some pictures of different levels to help you memorise the location of important items.

In the recent film Rush, James Hunt was seen physically rehearsing the gear changes and memorising the corners, not actually in his racing car, but before the race in his trailer – it just shows how powerful the human mind really is.

Thanks for reading. If you have purchased this book on Amazon then I would appreciate a review – constructive criticism of course and positive thoughts/comments.

www.johnbc.co.uk
www.radiojohnbc.com

# ABOUT THE AUTHOR

John Bates Clare, CT ABRSM is a professional Piano Teacher, Tuner and Pianist. He is a prolific blogger, championing Indie (Independent) music bands and artists. He has his own Internet Radio Station and has written one other work How to Really Pass A Piano Examination. John has been playing computer games since the age of eight. He is 43 and lives with his family in Lytham St Annes.